D. R. SHE

Old Mali and the Boy

Retold by John Milne

HEINEMANN ELT

Series Editor: John Milne

The Heinemann Elt Guided Readers provide a choice of enjoyable reading material for learners of English. The series is published at five levels – Starter, Beginner, Elementary, Intermediate and Upper. At **Intermediate Level**, the control of content and language has the following main features:

Information Control

Information which is vital to the understanding of the story is presented in an easily assimilated manner and is repeated when necessary. Difficult allusion and metaphor are avoided and cultural backgrounds are made explicit.

Structure Control

Most of the structures used in the Readers will be familiar to students who have completed an elementary course of English. Other grammatical features may occur, but their use is made clear through context and reinforcement. This ensures that the reading, as well as being enjoyable, provides a continual learning situation for the students. Sentences are limited in most cases to a maximum of three clauses and within sentences there is a balanced use of simple adverbial and adjectival phrases. Great care is taken with pronoun reference.

Vocabulary Control

There is a basic vocabulary of approximately 1,600 words. Help is given to the students in the form of illustrations, which are closely related to the text.

Glossary

Some difficult words and phrases in this book are important for understanding the story. Some of these words are explained in the story, some are shown in the pictures, and others are marked with a number like this...[3] Words with a number are explained in the Glossary on page 77.

Contents

A Note About This Story

This story is told by a young English boy who lived in a village in the hills in the north of India. The boy is called Jeffrey and he is twelve years old. His father is dead and Jeffrey lives in a small village with his mother. Jeffrey's mother is a teacher in the village elementary school. The elementary school is the school for young children.

Jeffrey and his mother live in a house which stands at the top of a little hill at the edge of the village. There is a large garden round the house and there is an Indian servant who works in the garden. Jeffrey does not know this servant's real name and he calls the servant Old Mali. Mali is the Indian word for gardener – a man who works in a garden. Mali cannot say Jeffrey's name correctly and he calls Jeffrey, 'Jeffa Baba'.

Old Mali has looked after Jeffrey ever since his father died. Jeffrey knows that Old Mali is a servant, but he also thinks of Old Mali as a friend. But above all Jeffrey thinks of Old Mali as an old man who tells him exciting stories.

Near to the village where Jeffrey lives is the jungle – hundreds of miles of thick forest. There are dangerous animals in the jungle. Most of Old Mali's stories are about hunting and killing these animals.

In this book Old Mali tells one of these exciting stories. These stories lead Old Mali and Jeffrey to try to live an adventure story in real life.

A Map of India

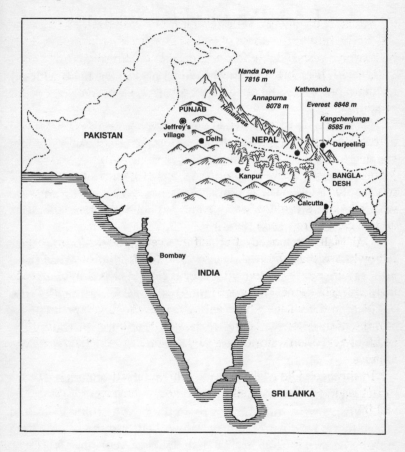

1

I Am Punished for Stealing

After school one day, I went out to play in the fields with my friends, Davy and Jerry. We were all about twelve years old at the time.

As we were playing, we saw some maize[1] growing in a field. The cobs looked ripe. We decided to pick some and make a fire and cook them.

We started to pick the cobs and put them inside our shirts. Suddenly we heard a shout. The farmer had seen us and was running towards us. We felt excited and ran away across the fields holding the cobs inside our shirts.

We escaped into a wood behind the fields and went to a place where no one could see us. We lit a fire carefully so that there was no smoke. Then we cooked the cobs on the fire and ate them with enjoyment. We did not think that we were stealing the cobs of maize.

Unfortunately, we were discovered. Everyone in the village knew me because my mother was a schoolteacher in the village elementary school.

The farmer had recognized me. He told the headmaster that we had stolen the cobs of maize.

When I went into the classroom the next morning I was told to go to the headmaster's office. When I entered the headmaster's office, he was sitting at his desk looking very angry. I knew immediately that I was in trouble.

'Where were you yesterday after school?' the headmaster asked in an angry voice.

'I was playing in the fields with Jerry and Davy,' I replied.

'Did you steal any cobs of maize?' the headmaster asked.

'Yes,' I replied. 'We took some cobs of maize and cooked them and ate them.'

'Didn't you know that you were stealing?' asked the headmaster, becoming even angrier.

I did not know what to say.

'You must be punished – you and Jerry and Davy,' said the
headmaster. 'You will be punished this afternoon at two o'clock in
the upstairs dormitory².'

At two o'clock I went upstairs with Davy and Jerry. We were
shaking with fear. But I did not want to show that I was afraid.

The headmaster stood beside a bed holding a hard-looking
cane in his right hand.

'You first,' he said, pointing to Jerry. 'Bend down and put your
hands on the bed.'

Jerry bent down over the bed and the headmaster hit him on
his bottom with the cane.

The headmaster beat him thirteen times. After the headmaster had hit him five times, Jerry was crying and screaming
louder and louder. By the time the headmaster had hit him for the
thirteenth time, Jerry was like a beaten dog.

Davy was next and he was much braver than Jerry. He did not
make a sound until he had been hit eight times.

I was the last to be beaten. When I had been hit eight times I
began to cry quietly.

Then, when we had all been beaten, the headmaster spoke to
us.

'You have behaved very, very badly,' he said. 'You have stolen
food from people who are poor and hungry. If you do it again, you
will be punished in front of the whole school.'

I walked down the stairs very slowly and very carefully. Usually,
when school was finished for the day, I ran home like the wind.
That day I walked home very slowly.

2

I Come Home From School

As I walked home, I thought about my mother. I did not feel ashamed because I still did not think we had been stealing. It had all been a game. But now I felt ashamed when I thought about my mother.

My mother would see the red marks on my legs where the cane had hit me. She would know that I had been punished and she would be angry.

As I was thinking about this, I came to our garden gate. Our house stood on top of a little hill beside the village. Steps went up from the road to our front door. There was a large garden on the hillside round the house. There were thirty-eight steps from the roadway to our house and I slowly began to climb up the steps, still feeling the pain from my beating.

As I was climbing the steps, I suddenly remembered Old Mali. I felt more ashamed. I did not want Old Mali to know that I had been punished.

Old Mali was our gardener and I loved him. Old Mali was very old. He was so old that he did not know his age.

I had always liked Old Mali because he told me stories. His stories were about himself when he was a young man. And every time, he told his stories in such a way that I felt that I was there with him taking part in his adventures.

Most of his stories were about hunting. When he was a young man, Mali had been a great hunter. He had hunted many animals in the jungle and had had many adventures. The stories that I liked best were the ones about his adventures when hunting.

One day, I wanted Old Mali to take me hunting with him in the jungle. He had promised to bring me his bow[3] which he had used when he was hunting. He had promised to let me see it and even touch it.

When I remembered the bow, I forgot all about my punishment. I felt much happier. Perhaps Old Mali would have brought the bow with him today. He had promised to bring it some time ago but he had always forgotten.

Then I saw him at the top of the garden digging with his spade.

I hurried over to him as fast as I could. I immediately asked him about the bow.

'Did you bring the bow today, Old Mali?' I asked excitedly.

He stopped digging and looked down at the ground. Whenever he looked at the ground in that way, I knew that there was something wrong. I realized that he had not brought the bow with him.

'Oh, Mali!' I cried in disappointment. 'You've forgotten it again.'

Old Mali slowly put his spade down and sat on the ground. On his head he wore a turban. His eyes moved quickly and were like a bird's. They seemed to see everything. His face was covered with lines. And, when he smiled, the lines seemed to become deeper.

When Old Mali was seated comfortably, he began to speak.

'Sit down, Jeffa Baba,' he said, 'and I will tell you why I forgot to bring the bow.'

'I don't think that I can sit down, Mali,' I replied.

'And why is that?' he asked.

I felt ashamed and looked down at the ground. Then I looked at his hands. They were old and covered with lines like his face. I was always interested in his right hand. The middle finger was missing and I knew the story of how he had lost that finger.

'I can't sit down,' I replied slowly, 'because the headmaster beat me this afternoon and my bottom is hurting.'

I felt ashamed again but now it was different. I could talk to Old Mali and he would understand. He would not think that I had done something wrong.

9

Old Mali sat on the ground. On his head he wore a turban.
His eyes moved quickly and were like a bird's.

'Why did the headmaster beat you?' Mali asked quietly.

'I don't know,' I replied. 'We took some maize cobs from a field and made a fire and ate them.'

Old Mali thought before he said anything.

'Where were the maize cobs when you took them, Jeffa Baba?' he asked after some time.

'In a field outside the village,' I replied defiantly.

'But those maize cobs didn't grow in that field by accident,' he said, after thinking quietly for some time. 'Someone worked hard, planting the maize and looking after it while it was growing. And so you really were stealing.'

For the first time that day I began to feel that perhaps I had done something wrong. I felt very ashamed and I began to cry.

'Don't cry Jeffa Baba,' said Old Mali to me very kindly. 'I remember when I was a young boy. I used to take maize cobs with my friends and we did not think that we were doing anything wrong. You will understand that only when you are older.'

When Old Mali said these words to me, I felt much happier and stopped crying. Perhaps I had done something wrong, but perhaps it did not matter.

Old Mali spoke again.

'Were you brave or did you cry when you were beaten?' he asked me.

'I cried a little but not loudly. I didn't cry like Jerry,' I replied.

'You were a brave boy,' said Old Mali. 'Now shall I tell you why I forgot to bring the bow?'

'No,' I replied. I had forgotten about the bow by this time. 'Please tell me the story about the bear again.'

I had heard Old Mali tell this story many times before. But I always wanted to hear it again. The story of the bear was one of Old Mali's most exciting stories. When he told me the story I always imagined that it was me and not Old Mali who was fighting with the bear.

'Well then,' replied Old Mali, 'lie on your side on the grass. If you lie that way, you won't feel the pain so much. And I will tell you of the time that I fought the trapped bear.'

3

Old Mali Tells a Story

I lay down carefully on my side in the place where the grass was thickest and I made myself comfortable.

While I was making myself comfortable on the grass, Old Mali took a box of matches from his shirt pocket. He lit a match and put the lighted match to his *beerie*[4] – the rolled tobacco leaf – and smoked the *beerie* slowly and carefully. When it was burning well, he relaxed.

He took the *beerie* out of his mouth, licked his lips and was ready to tell the story.

'One day, many years ago, when I was a young man . . .' began Old Mali.

All of Old Mali's stories began like that.

'One day, many years ago, when I was a young man, I went out hunting. I wanted to find some deer,' Old Mali continued.

'I left my village early in the morning and I walked through the fields straight into the jungle. I was carrying my bow over my left shoulder and I was holding my axe in my right hand as usual. My long, sharp *kukri*[5] was held firmly in my *dhoti*[6].

'I travelled many miles but did not see any deer,' the old man went on. 'The time was near midday. I knew that because the sun was moving overhead and because the jungle was becoming quieter. There are always some animals making noises in the jungle, but it is quietest at midday when the sun is hottest.

'One day, many years ago, when I was a young man,
I went out hunting.'

'Suddenly the silence was broken. There was a loud snapping noise in front of me. It was like a great set of steel teeth snapping together. Immediately I knew what it was. Some animal had walked into a trap and the trap had closed on the animal's leg.

'Have you seen a trap, Jeffa Baba?' asked Old Mali. He always called me Jeffa because he found it difficult to say my name correctly. He had called me Jeffa Baba since I was a small boy.

I told Old Mali that I had seen a trap. In fact I had seen many traps, but as usual Old Mali explained how the trap worked. Like all hunters, Old Mali had a great respect for such traps. Hunters were always afraid that their own legs would get caught in a trap.

'A trap has two edges of sharp steel teeth,' Old Mali explained. 'These steel teeth are kept open by a steel rod. If an animal – or a man – puts a leg in the trap, this rod is pushed away. Then the sharp teeth snap together. The steel teeth bite into the animal's leg and it cannot escape.'

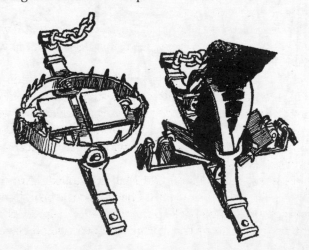

Old Mali stopped talking for a few moments. He lit another match and continued smoking his *beerie*. Then he went on with his story.

'Almost at the same time as I heard the loud, sharp snap,' Old Mali went on, 'I heard the terrible roaring of an animal in pain. I realized immediately that an animal had been caught in the trap. And from the strength and loudness of the roar, I knew that it must be a bear.

'I felt afraid,' said Old Mali quietly and simply.

Hunters do not often talk about being afraid. An angry bear is the most fearful thing in the jungle. Every hunter is afraid of a bear when it is really angry.

'I waited absolutely still and silent for a few minutes. Then there was another fearful roaring and I heard a loud tearing sound. The bear was obviously pulling at bushes and grass trying to escape.

'At last,' continued Old Mali, 'I felt brave enough to move forward. I crept quietly up the jungle path and soon I came to the edge of a clearing[7]. I stood behind a bush so that I was half hidden. And there in the clearing I saw a fearful sight.

'There was a bear standing in the clearing only a few metres away from me. Its leg was firmly fixed in a trap. The trap was held by a chain to a strong tree.

'I stood silently at the edge of the clearing,' went on Old Mali. 'I watched the bear pulling at the trap and then looking at it from time to time. It seemed to be trying to understand what had happened to its leg. Then it gave one strong pull and the pain in its leg got much worse. Its face twisted with anger and fear and pain and it roared loudly.

'I felt afraid once again,' Old Mali continued. 'And it was a fear that would not leave me until I had killed the bear. I knew that there was no time to go back to the village for help. By the time I brought help back from the village, the bear would have pulled itself free.'

Old Mali stopped for a few moments to light his *beerie* again and then he went on with his story.

'Also,' and now he spoke as if he had remembered something

'There was a bear standing only a few metres away from me.
Its leg was firmly fixed in a trap.'

that he had almost forgotten to put into the story. 'Also, there is a law among all the villages. A man who finds an animal caught in a trap kills it, shares the animal with the man who put the trap there and takes half of the animal.

'And as you know, Jeffa Baba,' continued Old Mali, 'bear's grease[8] is valuable. So I knew that I had to kill that bear. I stood at the edge of the clearing and wondered how I could get near enough to kill such a strong and angry animal.'

4

Mali Fights the Bear

While Old Mali was talking I lay back on the grass and shut my eyes. I tried to imagine that I was standing at the edge of the clearing. I wondered what I would do.

In my imagination, I became brave. I imagined myself running to the bear and killing it with my knife. In my imagination, I was so brave that I forgot completely how terrible and dangerous an angry bear could be.

Then Old Mali began to speak again and I listened.

'I moved into the clearing and made a loud noise,' Old Mali continued. 'When the bear saw me, it stood absolutely still for one second and stared at me with its red eyes. I stood still also, and tried not to feel frightened. Then suddenly the bear tried to pull itself free of the trap. It pulled angrily away from the trap. The trap rose in the air. But the chain was strong and the bear was pulled to the ground. When the bear hit the ground, it gave a loud roar of pain.

'I felt brave,' went on Old Mali, 'now that I knew how far the bear could move. I also knew that the chain was strong. I shouted rude words at the bear and this seemed to make it angrier than before. It stood up on its legs again and roared angrily.

'I stood back and wondered how I could kill such a large strong animal. The axe and the *kukri* were useless. If I tried to kill the bear with the axe or the *kukri*, the bear would kill me before I could kill it.

'Then I remembered the bow over my shoulders and the six arrows on my back. I decided to try to kill the bear using bow and arrows. But an arrow was not likely to go through the bear's thick body. The arrows were too thin and were made for killing deer not bears.

'I put my axe down beside me on the ground and took the bow from my shoulder. I fitted one of the arrows to the bow and looked up at the bear.

'I faced the bear and wondered where I should aim the arrow.

'I decided,' said Old Mali, as he went on with his story, 'to try to hit the bear so that the arrow went into its heart. But I knew that I had to hit the bear in its side.

'The bear stood facing me. I moved round in a circle to the right so that I could aim the arrow at the bear's side. But the bear seemed to understand what I was trying to do and moved round with me.

'We stood facing each other. The bear opened its mouth. Its huge teeth looked red and horrible. I knew that if the bear got to me it would tear me to pieces[9].

'I held the bow and arrow in my left hand and picked up a stone with my right hand. I threw the stone at the bear and hit it exactly on the nose. And as you know, Jeffa Baba,' said Old Mali, 'a bear feels pain in its nose more than anywhere else.

'When the stone hit the bear's nose, the bear let out another roar of pain and rage. The roar was louder than any I had heard before. The bear tried to run at me. It jumped up in the air and fell back heavily onto the ground.

'I raised up my bow and arrow. I held them with both hands and aimed at the bear's side. I let go of the arrow and it flew into the bear's body. But I had aimed too high. The arrow had gone in too near the bear's shoulder to injure the bear badly.'

'I quickly took another arrow, fitted it into the bow and fired. But the bear moved slightly as I fired. This arrow went into its chest. But it seemed to go in deeper than the first arrow.

'The bear stopped its roaring. It turned over and sat up on the ground. Then it looked at the arrow in its body. Suddenly the bear held the arrow with its paw and tried to pull it out. Then the bear gave another loud roar of pain and fell back silent on the ground.

'The bear lay there breathing very deeply. I immediately thought that the bear was dying. I dropped the bow to the ground and picked up the axe. I waited a few moments and then, holding the axe firmly in my right hand, I moved quickly towards the bear.

'The bear still lay on the ground breathing deeply. I raised the axe high above my head and moved round so that I could see the back of the bear's head. If I could hit the back of its head with all my strength, then I would be able to kill the bear.

'I moved a little closer and was now near enough to hit the bear's head. My right hand was shaking with fear because I was so near the bear. Suddenly I felt a terrible pain in my left leg and I fell over backwards. The axe flew out of my hand and hit a tree a few metres behind me.

'It took me a few moments to understand what had happened. The bear had not been seriously injured at all. It had just been resting and as soon as it had seen me within reach[10] it had hit at me with its paw.

'Luckily,' went on Old Mali, 'I had been pushed backwards and out of the bear's reach. The bear was on its feet again and trying to reach me with its long sharp claws.

'I lay back for some moments and gradually felt the pain in my left leg becoming greater and greater. I sat up and looked at my leg. Part of my leg was torn away and blood was pouring out of the wound. I took out a piece of strong string that I always carried with me. I tied this string tightly round my left leg above the knee. Then I twisted the string tightly to stop my leg bleeding.

'As I was busy doing this, the bear was still roaring and trying to reach me with its long arms. I turned over carefully on my stomach and crawled away from the bear.

'Then I turned back on my side again and sat up against a tree. I started to think about how I could kill that bear. I was more determined than ever to kill it. If I had not been thrown out of the bear's reach, it would have killed me.

'Then suddenly,' Old Mali continued, 'I had an idea. I staggered[11] up on my right leg and pulled out my *kukri*. I looked round and saw some tall bamboo canes. I moved slowly over to the bamboo canes. I chose a thick cane about four metres long and cut through it with my *kukri*.

'Then I sat down on the ground again and pulled one end of the bamboo cane towards me. I had chosen well because this cane was strong but not too heavy. I took a piece of thin rope that I had tied round my waist. Using this thin rope I tied my *kukri* very firmly to the end of the bamboo cane.

'I lifted myself up on to my right leg. I tried to put my left foot down on the ground but the pain was terrible. I staggered forwards towards the bear holding the bamboo cane in both hands.

'The bear saw me approaching with my *kukri* tied to the bamboo cane. It tried to reach out to the *kukri* and snatch it away. But I pulled the *kukri* back quickly and stood still and waited.

'The bear drew back and then made another rush at me. It

rushed towards me and again the trap pulled at its leg and it fell on the ground with a loud roar. I moved forward quickly and holding the long cane firmly in both hands I aimed it just behind the bear's left shoulder.

'I fell forward as I pushed and a great pain came into my injured leg. Luckily the point of the *kukri* pushed into the bear's shoulder and went deep into the bear's body.

'I struggled to hold firmly on to the cane and gave another strong push. I nearly fell forward into the bear's arms. I stopped myself from falling again by holding on to the cane. I gave a final push and threw myself back. Then I fell on the ground out of the bear's reach.

'I sat up on the ground,' Old Mali went on, 'and sat watching the bear. I hoped that the point of my *kukri* had reached the bear's heart.

'For one moment, that seemed like an hour, the bear did not move. Suddenly it roared with rage and fear and threw itself high in the air. Then it crashed down on the ground for the last time. The bear was dead.'

5

Old Mali's Promise

Old Mali sat silently for a few moments. Then he continued the story. He told me of the long, terrible journey back to the village through steep jungle paths. He told me how his leg was still covered in blood and how it hurt him every time he moved.

'I staggered back to the place where the bamboo canes were growing,' said Old Mali. 'I found my axe on the ground and picked it up. Then I cut two strong canes with my axe. I cut them so that they were long enough to reach from the ground to under my shoulders. I used these canes to help me walk and I started the journey back to my village.

'It was a long, slow journey. Sometimes I thought I was going to fall down and die on the jungle path. In some places the path was so steep that I had to lie down on the ground and pull myself up the path, pulling my two bamboo canes behind me.

'When at last I reached the village,' continued Old Mali, 'all the men and women ran towards me. I was just able to tell them about the bear and about the place where I had killed it. Then I collapsed.

'I lay in my hut for almost three months before the leg got better,' the old man said. 'And when I was able to walk again there was a long scar on my leg which I have to this day.'

'Can I see the scar again?' I asked eagerly as I always did when he came to the end of the story.

Old Mali lifted up his *dhoti* and showed me his leg. I stared for some moments at the long scar on his thin left leg. Then I lay back on the grass and tried to imagine his long tiring journey through the jungle back to his village.

Then I remembered where I was and the beating that I had had in the morning. The pain in my leg became a real pain. I thought again about the beating and the pain I had felt. I remembered how I had wanted to cry.

'Did the pain in your leg make you cry?' I asked the old man.

'No,' he replied simply. 'A pain in the leg does not make a man cry.'

'Does a brave man ever cry?' I asked him.

'In my village,' replied Old Mali, 'there was a young girl that I loved. When I was lying on my bed waiting for my leg to get better, I heard that she had become very ill. A few days later they told me that she was dead. When I heard that she had died, I felt a great pain in my heart. Then I cried and cried for many hours.

'That is a time when even the bravest man can cry,' said

Old Mali.

I was too young to understand this. My father had died when I was very young and I did not remember anything about his death.

I was going to ask more questions about death, but Old Mali had heard enough of my questions. He stood up, picked up the spade and started to dig again in the garden.

I stood up too. The sun was moving down to the west and I knew that it was time to go into the house. It was nearly supper time and my mother would be waiting for me.

'You won't tell Mother that I was punished in school, will you, Mali?' I asked him.

Old Mali promised that he would not tell anyone about the beating. I trusted him completely because when he promised something, he always kept his promise[12]. Except about bringing the bow. I wondered why he always forgot to bring the bow with him.

'And what about the bow, Mali?' I asked him. 'Will you remember to bring the bow with you tomorrow?'

Old Mali stopped digging and thought for some moments before he replied.

'Yes,' he finally answered. 'I will bring the bow with me tomorrow.'

He looked at me for some moments. He seemed to be deciding how tall I was and how long my arms were. Then he finally spoke.

'The bow may be too big for you,' he said. 'If your arms are not strong enough to pull the bow, we may have to cut it down a little.

'But I don't want to cut the bow,' he went on, 'I remember making it when I was a young man. It took me hours to make.'

'But I will be strong enough,' I cried out loudly. 'I will use all my strength and pull it. Don't worry, Mali, you will not have to cut the bow.'

'Then the bow is yours,' Old Mali said simply.

He had made the decision. He was too old to use the bow now

and he was going to give it to me.

'Do you mean that you are going to give me the bow to keep?' I asked him. I was so pleased that I could not really believe what he had said.

'Of course you can keep the bow,' Old Mali replied. 'I have promised to give it to you. You will have it tomorrow morning. Now it is time for you to go home. Your mother will be waiting for you.'

Just as he said this, there was a loud shout from our house at the top of the hill.

'Jeff . . . rey.' It was my mother calling.

I turned and started to run up the hill. Then I stopped suddenly and turned back to Old Mali. 'You won't forget to bring the bow, will you?' I shouted to him.

'Get home quickly or you will get another beating,' he replied with a laugh.

Then I heard my mother shouting again.

'Jeff . . . rey, Jeff . . . rey, where are you?' she shouted.

'I'm coming, Mother. I'm coming,' I shouted in reply.

6

The Bow and Arrows

After supper I got into bed. I went to sleep quickly with my head full of thoughts about the bow.

Next morning, before it was daylight, I woke up. I was very excited about getting the bow. I got out of bed and put on my clothes in the half dark. I got dressed very quietly because I did not want my mother to hear me.

It was far too early for breakfast. Mother would still be asleep. And so I decided to walk along the path that led to Old Mali's village. He was always up early and I would be sure to meet him half-way. He would be bringing the bow with him and I would be able to meet him and see the bow.

I wanted to get out of the house quietly. I was afraid that my mother would order me to go back to bed. So I did not put my shoes on but carried them downstairs under my arm. When I was out of the house, I put on my shoes and started to walk along the road.

I walked past the church and the village elementary school where my mother was the schoolteacher. Then I left the road and walked along the forest path that led to Old Mali's village. I was sure that I would meet Old Mali coming along this path on his way to our house.

At last, as the daylight was becoming brighter, I saw Old Mali coming slowly towards me along the wet forest path. I hurried towards him and when he saw me coming he stood still.

'You have come early this morning,' said Old Mali with a laugh. 'You must be expecting something.'

'You haven't brought the bow,' I replied. And my voice showed that I was terribly disappointed.

'What do you think that this is then?' asked Old Mali, holding out a long, flat stick.

The stick that he held in his hand did not look like a bow. It was flat and very black in colour. And at one end of the stick there was a dirty looking piece of string tied round it.

'But, Mali,' I cried out, 'that's not a bow. That's only a piece of wood.'

'This is not a piece of wood, Jeffa Baba,' replied Old Mali. And I knew from the way that he spoke that Old Mali was disappointed too. He was disappointed because I had thought that the stick he held in his hand was not a bow.

'This is a piece of the best and strongest bamboo that grows in

I saw Old Mali coming slowly towards me along the wet forest path.

the deepest jungle,' Old Mali went on to explain.

'But how can that be bamboo cane?' I asked in amazement. 'Everyone knows that bamboo canes are round and that piece of wood in your hand is flat.'

As we were talking, Old Mali had loosened the piece of string on one end of the stick. As he loosened it, I realized that the piece of string was in fact a strong piece of leather. Then he pressed one end of the stick into the ground against his foot.

Old Mali pressed on the other end of the stick with all his strength. Slowly, as Old Mali pressed harder and harder, the stick began to bend. When it was bent over enough, Old Mali quickly tied the other end of the piece of leather to the top end of the stick.

Then Old Mali stood upright and gave me the bow. And it really was a bow now. It was the biggest and strongest bow that I had ever seen.

'You see, Jeffa Baba,' Old Mali explained, 'in the deepest part of the jungle, far away towards the Himalayas, there are bamboo canes that grow as thick as a man's body. This bow that you are holding was cut from a bamboo that was thicker than you are. Then it was burnt slowly in a thousand fires to make it as hard as iron. That is why it is flat and not round. And that, also, is why it is so black.'

Old Mali stopped talking suddenly because he realized that I was not listening. I had the bow in my hands and I was trying to pull the piece of leather and bend the bow. But I was not strong enough and could not bend the bow.

'Yes,' said Old Mali, 'I was afraid of that. The bow is too big for you. We will have to cut a piece from one end so that it is small enough for you to use.'

'No, no,' I cried. 'Look, it's bending now.'

And pulling with all my strength, I was able to pull the piece of leather so that the bow bent a little.

'Please don't cut the bow, Mali,' I said eagerly. 'I will go on trying until I am strong enough to make it bend.'

Old Mali did not reply. He saw how determined I was to use the bow and he said no more about it.

Then I remembered something that I had forgotten all about.

'But what about arrows, Mali?' I asked. 'You haven't brought any with you.'

'I haven't used the bow for many years,' replied Old Mali. 'All the arrows that I had have been lost. You will have to make some for yourself.'

'But you can make some arrows for me later today,' I replied. I did not realize that Old Mali was telling me to make the arrows.

'I have my work to do in the garden,' replied Old Mali seriously. 'Your mother pays me to work in the garden and I must do my work.

'Anyway, Jeffa Baba,' went on Old Mali, 'you must remember that arrows are easily lost in the jungle. If I make the arrows for you now, who will make them for you later? While I am alive, I can make arrows for you. But who will make arrows for you when I am dead?'

I looked down at the ground. Suddenly I felt sad. The sadness was the same feeling that I had had the day before, when Old Mali had spoken about the death of the woman that he had loved. Old Mali was so old. I did not think that he would ever die. Death was something that I did not understand and did not want to think about.

'It is you who must learn to make arrows,' Old Mali continued. 'Then when I am not beside you, you can always make arrows when you need them. And it takes time to make good arrows. You cannot make them in half an hour.'

I felt ashamed of my impatience and realized that Old Mali was right. I had to wait until I had time to go with him and learn how to make the arrows.

While we were talking, we had started to walk back towards our village and my house. When we came to the end of the forest path, we stepped out onto the road that ran round the village into bright sunshine. Then I remembered the sunshine holiday.

'If the sun is shining at nine o'clock this morning,' I explained to Old Mali, 'we will get a holiday from school. Then I can come with you to make the arrows.' Old Mali thought carefully for a few moments before replying. Then he spoke.

'I will do as much work in the garden as I can,' he said.

'And if you get a holiday today we can go and make the arrows.'

Old Mali was smiling. I felt happy and began to look up at the sky. I wished that all the clouds would disappear completely. I had never wanted anything so much in my life as I wanted a sunshine holiday on that day.

———

When I arrived at school that morning, all the boys were standing together in the courtyard. They were all talking excitedly. We were hoping that the headmaster would give us a holiday.

The sun was still shining and it was nearly nine o'clock. Suddenly all the boys became silent. The headmaster was standing on the steps that led up to the main door.

'You are very lucky today,' said the headmaster in a loud, clear voice. 'The sun is shining brightly and you can have a holiday.'

We all cheered loudly and began to run towards the school gate.

'Do you want to come fishing with us?' Jerry shouted.

'No thank you, I'm too busy today,' I shouted in reply. Then I rushed out of the gate and started to run home.

When I arrived at the steps leading up to the house, Old Mali was busy in the garden, planting some flowers. I went to talk to him.

'Mali, can we go to make the arrows now?' I asked eagerly.

'I must finish planting these flowers first,' he replied. 'If they are not planted today, they will die.'

And so I had to wait until he had finished his work.

When Old Mali had finished planting the flowers, I wanted to leave immediately. But Old Mali stopped me.

'Before we go into the forest,' said Old Mali, 'we must find a knife and some grease to take with us. We need a knife to cut the arrows and some grease to harden them.'

When we had found a sharp knife and some grease, we set out together. We walked into the forest for about half an hour. Then Old Mali suddenly stopped. He stood in front of a young tree with some strong branches on it.

'How many arrows do you want, Jeffa Baba?' Old Mali asked me, pointing to the strong straight branches.

'Ten,' I replied, saying the first number I thought of.

Old Mali laughed.

'You will have six,' he said. 'We will need all day to make six and that is enough.

'Now, Jeffa,' went on Old Mali. 'I want you to light a fire carefully. Use dry wood to start the fire but collect plenty of cryptomeria[13] to put on later. Cryptomeria will make plenty of smoke which we will need later to harden the arrows.'

While I was lighting the fire and collecting the cryptomeria, I watched Old Mali cut six branches into six pieces of wood of equal length and thickness. Then Old Mali looked at each one to make sure that it was straight and strong.

When the fire was burning brightly, I put some of the cryptomeria onto the fire and the hot smoke rose up in great clouds.

'Now watch what I do,' said Old Mali.

I bent down near the fire and watched Old Mali carefully. He placed the six arrows over the fire. Every few minutes when the fire started to burn too fiercely, Old Mali put on some more cryptomeria to make more smoke.

After the arrows were blackened all round, he took them off the fire and rubbed away the outer wood with his hands. Then he took some grease and rubbed it into the arrows one by one.

When Old Mali had made sure that each arrow was completely covered with the grease, he carefully put the arrows back over the fire. Then he sat back and waited.

'Now,' said Old Mali, 'what happens is that the heat and smoke dry up the water in the branches. The grease gets into the wood and hardens the arrows.'

'How long does it take?' I asked impatiently, as usual.

'Oh, it takes a long time – many hours,' he replied.

'Well, tell me a story while we are waiting,' I said immediately.

'And what story do you want me to tell you?' Old Mali asked.

He got out his *beerie* and lit it. He relaxed a little but was still sitting up near the fire and turning the arrows every few minutes.

'Tell me the story of how you killed the trapped bear,' I replied after a little thought.

'One day, many years ago,' Old Mali began as usual, 'when I was a young man, I went out hunting.'

I lay back in the long grass and listened once more to his story. I wondered when I would be old enough to go out hunting. Perhaps one day Old Mali would take me with him to go hunting in the jungle.

7

I Shoot My First Arrow

Much later in the afternoon, Old Mali decided that the arrows were finished. He took them off the fire and made sure that each arrow was straight and hard.

'Yes, the arrows are nearly ready, Jeffa Baba,' Old Mali said at last. 'Now we can go home and finish making the arrows.'

'What else do we need to do?' I asked impatiently. I wanted to

When Old Mali had made sure that each arrow was covered
with the grease, he put the arrows back over the fire.

put the arrows in the bow and shoot them off immediately.

'Firstly,' said Old Mali, 'you must have feathers fitted at one end of each arrow to make it fly straight. Do you have any feathers at home that we could use?'

'Yes,' I replied eagerly. 'I have some at home.'

'And I have some strong string to tie the feathers tightly,' said Old Mali. 'I also have some resin to cover the string. Resin is a kind of wax. It will harden the string and stop the feathers from falling out. That is all we need. You can go now and get the feathers. I will meet you at the bottom of the garden.'

I rushed off ahead of Old Mali, straight up the garden steps and to my bedroom. I found some feathers from an old hat and brought them down with me. Then I went into the garden where Old Mali was sitting.

He took the feathers and tied them with string to the end of each arrow. Then he covered the string with resin.

Now I thought that the arrows were ready to use. I picked up one arrow in my right hand and the bow in my left hand.

'Not yet, not yet,' said Old Mali as I tried to fit the arrow to the bow. 'We must leave the arrows until tomorrow so that the resin will harden over the feathers.'

'Can't I try just one?' I asked Old Mali anxiously.

Old Mali could see how much I wanted to shoot an arrow from the bow.

'All right, Jeffa,' he said, 'you can shoot one arrow, once only.'

I fitted the arrow into the bow. Then I pointed the bow and arrow high up the side of the garden and let the arrow fly.

I fell back as I let go of the arrow and I did not see my arrow flying through the air. I looked up at the side of the garden but I could see nothing. I felt very disappointed and was sure that the arrow had dropped at my feet.

'Look! Up there!' laughed Old Mali.

I dropped the bow and rushed up the hill to get my arrow back.

When I returned, Old Mali had picked up the bow and was feeling it lovingly with his hands.

'Here, Mali, you have a try,' I said, giving him the arrow.

Old Mali did not want to use the arrow because he had told me to use it once only. But I told him that I very much wanted to see him shooting an arrow. In the end, he could not refuse. He took the arrow and fitted it to the bow.

Slowly Old Mali pulled back the arrow. He pulled it back much further than I had done. When he let go, the arrow shot up high into the air. At first, I could see nothing. Then I saw the bright red feathers in the air. Old Mali's arrow was flying twice as high as mine. When it came down, it was forty metres away high up on the side of the garden.

'Oh, Mali!' I shouted with joy. 'That was a wonderful shot. Will I ever be able to shoot an arrow as far as that?'

'With patience and plenty of practice,' Old Mali replied, 'you will be able to shoot an arrow much further than I ever could. But now it's nearly supper time and you must go. There will be no sunshine holiday tomorrow. You must get ready for school.'

When Old Mali spoke about the sunshine holiday, I remembered that the day was over. I had to go back to school the next day. But there would be another holiday quite soon. This next holiday would last a whole week.

Then a wonderful idea came into my mind.

'Mali,' I said suddenly, 'we have seven days' holiday quite soon. Why can't I go hunting with you?'

Old Mali looked amazed when I told him my idea. He was very old now and had not been out hunting for many years. He stood and thought about my idea for some time.

'But what would we hunt?' he asked at last.

I did not know what to say. Then I remembered the beginning of the story about the trapped bear.

'Why, deer, of course,' I said. 'We can go and hunt deer.'

'But the deer are many miles away in the jungle,' replied Old

Mali. 'It would take us a whole day's journey to find any deer. And we would have to sleep two nights in the jungle.

'No, it's quite impossible,' Old Mali continued, after thinking in silence for some moments. 'You would have to be away from home for three whole days. Your mother would never allow that. And, anyway, you would not be able to walk far enough in one day to reach the deer. We must wait until you are a few years older.'

Old Mali started to get ready to go home. I picked up the bow and arrows.

'Carry the arrows carefully,' Old Mali warned me.

I promised Old Mali that I would take care of the arrows. I said goodnight to him and walked up the steps to the house.

Old Mali thought that I had forgotten my idea of going hunting with him. But I had not forgotten it. Now that the idea had come into my mind, I was determined to go. I would talk to Mother about it and then persuade Old Mali to take me with him.

I would really live the life that Old Mali described in his stories.

8

We Go into the Jungle

Every time I met my mother, I spoke to her about the journey into the jungle. At first she laughed. She thought that it was a childish idea of mine and that I would soon forget it.

Every evening I spoke to Old Mali. He repeated what he had said before. He said that I would not be able to walk far enough. Also, he said that my mother would not allow me to go.

As the days of the holiday came nearer, I reminded Old Mali of his stories about hunting. I asked him how old he had been when he first went hunting in the jungle. I learnt that Old Mali had been a very young boy when he first went hunting. In fact, he had been younger than I was when he first went into the jungle.

Also, I reminded my mother that I was growing older. Soon I would want to go away on my own or with other boys from school. I asked her if it would not be better for me to go on my first journey into the jungle with Old Mali. I told her that Old Mali would look after me. He would teach me all that I needed to know.

Also, I practised with the bow and arrow every day. After a few days I was able to use it properly. I could aim at and hit a mark on a tree about twenty-five metres away. It was this ability to use the bow and arrow that at last persuaded Old Mali to take me with him into the jungle.

In the end, Old Mali and my mother had a long talk together. They agreed that I could go with Old Mali to hunt in the jungle.

We began our journey on the third day of the holiday. Old Mali spent the night in a hut in the garden. We were all out of bed a long time before daylight. The moon was shining brightly as Mother said goodbye to us at the front door of the house.

Mother looked as if she might start crying. I thought that at the last minute she might change her mind and refuse to let me go. So I said goodbye quickly, and Old Mali and I went down the steps towards the road.

We passed the church and the village elementary school in the moonlight. Then we entered the beginning of the jungle where it was still quite dark. We did not go by the forest path which led to Old Mali's village. Instead, we entered by another path. This path led straight off from the road that passed by our village. From the moment we entered the jungle I felt lost. Old Mali walked in front because he knew the way and I followed behind him.

After we had walked for about three miles, I began to feel tired. Old Mali was carrying the bow and arrows and a small bag. I was carrying my rucksack. It was full of food. There was also a blanket

37

Old Mali was carrying the bow and arrows and a small bag.
I was carrying my rucksack.

in the rucksack. I had tried to tell Mother that I did not need a blanket in the jungle. I was going to make my own bed, but she would not let me go without taking the blanket.

The weight of the rucksack and the darkness of the forest path were making me feel quite tired. I began to think that perhaps Old Mali was right after all. Perhaps I would not be able to walk far enough to reach the deer. I could see Old Mali looking round at me every now and again. Probably he was thinking the same as me. He was probably wondering if the journey was going to be too far for me and if we would have to turn back.

But I walked on without saying a word. As the sun came up and the path became clearer, I felt much better. The rucksack seemed to get lighter and I followed on behind Old Mali.

After about two hours' walking, we stopped in a little clearing beside a stream.

'Now we can rest,' said Old Mali. 'Take off your rucksack and rest your back.'

I took off my rucksack and dropped it on the ground. Then I lay down on the grass and stretched out completely. Old Mali laid down the bow and arrows on the ground and sat down beside them. He took out a *beerie*, lit it and started to smoke.

After about five minutes, I sat up and got some sandwiches out of the rucksack. I started to eat the sandwiches. I offered Old Mali one of my sandwiches but he refused.

As I sat eating my sandwiches, I thought how little I knew about Old Mali. I wondered who made his food and how much he ate every day. I knew that my mother often gave him food to take home with him in the evening. I wondered if he was often hungry.

We stayed in the clearing for half an hour. Then I packed everything back in my rucksack and we moved on again. The jungle was getting thicker. There was a green wall of trees and leaves ahead of us. I had never been so far in the jungle in my life before. I had no idea of the path back home. I had to follow Old Mali wherever he went.

'Will we find some deer in there?' I asked Old Mali.

'No, not yet,' he laughed. 'We must go much further before we find any deer. Don't you remember? We must walk for one full day and sleep one night before we will see any deer.'

'How many deer will we see when we get there?' I asked Old Mali. 'Will we see ten – or perhaps twenty?'

'No, not nearly so many,' Old Mali replied. 'In all my life I have never seen more than five deer at one time.'

'But why will we see only five?' I asked with a feeling of disappointment. I wanted to see lots of deer – far more than twenty.

'I do not know why we will not see more than five,' answered Old Mali. 'All I know is that in my whole life I have never seen more than five deer together. I do not think that it will be different tomorrow.'

We walked on for another three hours until it was midday. It was much more difficult to walk now. Sometimes we had to crawl up a steep slope. At other times the leaves and branches were so thick that we had to push our way through them.

When it was twelve o'clock and the sun was high above us, we rested under a huge tree. The jungle had become much quieter at midday, just as Old Mali had described it in his stories.

I lay down on the soft ground. It was covered with dead leaves and no grass grew there at all. Suddenly there was a noise in the bushes at the foot of the tree. Something had moved. I jumped to my feet holding my knife in my hand. Old Mali jumped up too.

'What was it that disturbed you?' Old Mali asked.

'I don't know,' I replied. 'Something moved in the bushes. Perhaps it was a snake.'

The noise in the bushes stopped and I lay down again to rest. Old Mali also sat down again, and seemed to fall into a half sleep.

I was surprised by the way Old Mali had suddenly jumped to his feet. I wondered if Old Mali was afraid of anything. Then I realized that Old Mali felt a great responsibility for me. He was worried and afraid that something might happen to me.

9

A Night in the Jungle

Once again, we moved on into the jungle. Old Mali went in front carrying his axe and I followed close behind him. There was no clear path now. The path was covered over with branches and bushes. I had no idea where I was. Without Old Mali in front of me, I would be lost completely.

We stopped for the night about an hour before it started to get dark. We put our bags on the ground in a small clearing. There was a stream at the edge of the clearing and we could get our drinking water from the stream.

Old Mali lit a fire. When it was alight, he showed me how to make a bed. He arranged a great pile of cryptomeria and covered the top with soft moss. Then he helped me make my bed on the other side of the fire.

When I had covered the cryptomeria with plenty of moss, I lay down on my bed. It was soft and comfortable.

'Mali', I said, 'this bed is more comfortable than my bed at home.'

Old Mali just laughed quietly in reply.

'But how did you learn to make such a bed, Mali?' I asked.

'I learnt to make beds like that,' Old Mali replied, 'by watching and listening to others. That is the real way to learn anything.'

'Will you let me watch you always?' I asked Old Mali. 'I want to learn all the things that you know about the jungle.'

'You won't learn anything if you are lazy and lie in your bed all the time,' was Old Mali's reply. 'Who do you think is going to collect the wood for the fire? We need enough wood to keep the fire going all night. Will I have to do it all by myself?'

I jumped up quickly, feeling ashamed.

'No, of course not. I will help you,' I replied quickly.

Then I realized that Old Mali was laughing at me. He did not really think that I was lazy. He felt proud that I wanted to learn from him.

We went off together into the jungle to collect as much wood as possible.

'We must have some large pieces of wood,' Old Mali said.

'They last longer and the fire must stay lit all night. We must have a fire to keep away any animals that come near. All animals are afraid of fire.'

It was almost dark by the time we had collected a huge pile of firewood. We put the wood beside Old Mali's bed so that he could reach it easily during the night. He would be able to pick up the wood and put it on the fire without getting out of his bed.

We sat down beside the fire to eat our supper. I opened a tin of meat and a tin of beans. I started to eat the meat and beans with a whole loaf of bread. I felt glad that as I ate the food I was making my rucksack lighter. It would not be so heavy to carry on the next day.

Old Mali took out some Indian food. I had nearly finished my meal before I thought of Old Mali. Then I wished that I had not eaten so much. I realized that he did not have very much food with him.

I offered Old Mali the little piece of meat that was left in the tin. He thanked me and ate it all up.

When we had finished our supper, Old Mali got onto his bed of cryptomeria and moss and lay down. It was now completely dark. In the firelight Old Mali seemed to be fast asleep on his bed. I suddenly felt alone and afraid. I wished that Old Mali would wake up and share my loneliness.

All day in the jungle, while we were walking, I had heard noises of animals. Now they seemed to be much nearer. The jungle was now a wall of blackness in the light of the fire. From far away in this blackness I heard the crying of a jackal. I remembered many stories about jackals. They are animals that look like dogs. All hunters are afraid of the bite from a mad jackal. They say that if someone is bitten by a mad jackal then that person will go mad. I wondered if this was a mad jackal crying in the night.

I felt frightened and suddenly my mouth went dry. I really wished that Old Mali would wake up to share my fear. I wanted to scream. I felt my mouth opening wide, ready to scream out as loudly as possible.

I breathed deeply and was just about to scream out in fear. But I did not scream. I saw Old Mali's face in the firelight. This made me feel ashamed. If I screamed, Old Mali would know that I was afraid.

I held my teeth tightly together to stop myself from screaming. I lay down on my comfortable bed of cryptomeria and moss and closed my eyes.

As soon as I closed my eyes, I heard a thousand noises. The whole jungle became alive with animals creeping all round me. Suddenly Old Mali took a deep breath and made a noise. I was hearing so many imaginary noises, that the real noise made by Old Mali gave me a terrible fright.

I opened my eyes and jumped out of bed. I pulled my *kukri* out and held it above my head. I was sure that I was going to see a mad jackal beside the fire.

All I saw was Old Mali who was now lying on his side with his eyes wide open.

'Hello, what is this then?' he asked, when he saw me on my feet beside the fire with my *kukri* in my hand.

'Oh, Mali,' I whispered thankfully, 'you are awake now!'

'Yes,' replied Old Mali, 'I must have fallen asleep for a few

I opened my eyes and jumped out of bed.

moments.

'And what are you doing with your knife out?' Old Mali asked.

I am sure that he knew that I had been afraid and had jumped out of my bed in fear. But as always, he was kind to me and pretended not to notice that I was afraid.

'You made a noise in your sleep,' I replied. 'I did not know what the noise was and I jumped out of bed to find out.'

'Well, you can put your knife away now,' said Old Mali quietly and calmly. 'It is time to go to sleep. You have a long day in front of you tomorrow. Remember you are going to hunt the deer.'

Old Mali's quiet and calm voice made me feel better. I got back into bed and lay down. I closed my eyes and, knowing that Old Mali was watching, I soon fell asleep.

10

I Kill a Monkey

When I woke early the next morning, Old Mali was already up. He was siting by the fire warming himself.

The large pile of wood which we had collected the night before was almost gone. Old Mali must have been putting the wood on the fire all night. I felt ashamed that I had slept so well. I had not woken up once.

Old Mali turned and saw that I was awake.

'Now,' Old Mali said, 'we must try and find the deer.'

When he spoke about the deer, I felt excited. I forgot about the fire and my fear of the night before. We put out the fire and got ready to move off.

There was a difference this time, however. Old Mali still walked in front, but now he was carrying my rucksack as well as his own bag. I was carrying the bow. I was ready to shoot an arrow as soon as I saw a deer.

Soon after we began walking Old Mali turned round and spoke to me.

'Now we must move silently,' he said. 'And we do not talk.'

'Yes, Mali,' I whispered at once in reply.

'One thing Mali,' I whispered to him again.

'Yes, what is it?' he replied.

'If the deer is near enough, I will shoot at it,' I said. 'But, if the deer is far away, I will pass the bow and arrow to you.'

'All right,' replied Old Mali. 'I will do whatever you want.'

I could use the bow well at short distances. But if the deer was too far away I would not be able to hit it. Old Mali would have to shoot the arrow if the deer was too far away.

I walked on in silence feeling very excited. Old Mali went in front and I walked carefully behind him. From time to time, Old Mali stopped and I stopped too. When he stopped, he looked all around him. He looked to the left and then to the right. Then he searched the bushes and trees in front of him.

I wondered if Old Mali was trying to smell the deer. I wondered what kind of smell a deer had. I asked myself if a deer smelt like a dog when it got wet in the rain. But I did not ask Old Mali any questions. I remembered that we were hunting for deer and must not talk.

I continued to follow Old Mali in silence. I stopped when he stopped and moved when he moved. At every moment I expected him to suddenly stop and show me lots of deer. In my imagination I expected to see far more than twenty deer. But we moved on slowly and time passed and we saw nothing.

When the sun was right overhead, Old Mali stopped and turned round.

'Well,' he said, 'there aren't any deer at all. I'm afraid that we will have to try and find some deer another day.'

I did not completely understand what he meant.

'We can hunt again after we have eaten our lunch, can't we Mali?' I asked impatiently.

'No,' Old Mali replied, 'that is enough for today. Now we must start to get back home. We have a long way to go.'

'But we can't go back yet,' I replied. 'We haven't seen any deer. And you promised me that we would see at least five.'

'Do not try to change my words, Jeffa Baba,' replied Old Mali patiently. 'I said that we would not see more than five. But I did not promise that we would see any at all.

'Now we have hunted all morning,' continued Old Mali, 'and it is time to return. I promised your mother that you would be back in three days. Tomorrow is the third day.'

When we were leaving home, I had been so eager to hunt the deer that I had not thought about returning.

'Mother will not worry if we are one day late,' I replied eagerly. 'The holiday lasts for another three days yet. Let us go on and hunt for the deer after lunch.'

'I made a promise to your mother,' Old Mali replied. He was now becoming impatient with me. 'I told her that I would bring you back on the third day and I am going to do that.

'It does not matter whether your mother will worry or not,' Old Mali continued. 'What matters is the promise that I made to her. And I am going to keep that promise. And, anyway, I know that she will worry. Even now she is worrying and wondering if you are safe. Do you want her to worry about you?

'Now it is time to return,' Old Mali said finally. He spoke in a very quiet and determined way. I knew that I was wrong but I still wanted to shoot an arrow at a deer.

'Can I keep the bow and arrows?' I asked him.

'Yes, you can keep the bow and arrows,' Old Mali replied. 'And now we will turn back.'

We continued walking through the jungle. I was completely lost. I did not even know that we had turned round. I realized that there were many things that I had to learn about the jungle. I would not be able to go on my own in the jungle until I knew much more about it.

We walked for about an hour and a half. I was still walking behind and Old Mali was walking in front. I was going more slowly now and Old Mali was about fifteen paces in front of me.

Suddenly I saw a group of monkeys. There were five of them. They were sitting round the huge roots of an old tree that had fallen down. They were picking at the roots for food.

Suddenly I wanted to use my bow and arrow. I had wanted so much to shoot an arrow at a deer. Now I just wanted to shoot an arrow at any living thing. I felt in me the desire that all men have, to hunt and kill an animal.

I raised my bow and fitted an arrow to the bow. I chose the biggest monkey to shoot at. The monkey seemed to know what I was doing. It stood up on its legs and stared at me.

I felt excited. I could only just breathe as I held the shaking bow and pointed it towards the monkey. I felt inside me a great desire to kill the monkey. I pulled back the bow with all my strength and then let go of the arrow. The arrow flew straight and went fiercely into the monkey's stomach.

The sound of the bow and the heavy sound of the arrow hitting the monkey made Old Mali stop immediately. He came running back quickly to see what I had done.

'Oh, no!' he cried out in horror. 'You haven't hit a monkey, have you?'

'I've killed it, Mali!' I shouted out. My voice was full of the madness of killing. 'Look, I've killed him!'

Old Mali held me tightly and started to shake me. For a moment he was angrier with me than he had ever been. Then he stopped shaking me and stood back.

I was amazed at the anger which Old Mali had shown. I had never seen him so angry. I did not understand what I had done wrong. I had only killed a monkey. Old Mali seemed calmer now. He explained quietly and gently what I had done wrong.

Suddenly I saw a group of monkeys. They were sitting round the huge roots of an old tree that had fallen down.

'It is very unlucky to kill a monkey,' Old Mali explained. 'All hunters believe that it is bad luck to kill a monkey. I have never shot an arrow at a monkey.

'But I cannot blame you,' Old Mali continued. 'It is my fault. I should have told you about it. I should have warned you never to shoot an arrow at a monkey.'

I felt very sad and worried. I had done something really wrong. There was so much that I had to learn about the jungle.

Then the monkey suddenly started moaning. I looked at it and saw, with horror, that it was still alive. It was sitting up and trying to pull the arrow out of its stomach.

The monkey pulled at the arrow until the arrow came out of its stomach. It threw the arrow away and started to pull at the wound with its paws. I stared with horror as the inside of the monkey's stomach began to come out.

It was a terrible sight but I could not stop looking at the monkey. I felt sick. The monkey was now pulling out the whole of its stomach and moaning with pain.

'It is looking for the reason for the pain,' Old Mali explained to me gently. 'It is a bad thing to leave an animal in pain like that. I must kill it.'

Old Mali raised his axe and moved towards the monkey. He was going to kill the monkey to free it from its pain. I could not stop looking at the monkey. I was not watching Old Mali.

Suddenly there was a loud snapping noise and Old Mali began screaming. My eyes moved away from the monkey and looked round at Old Mali. Old Mali had fallen over and was crying with pain.

At first I thought that he had just fallen over. I expected him to stand up again. But, as he lay there with cries of pain, I realized that something terrible had happened.

I rushed over to where he was lying. I looked down and saw what had happened. Old Mali's leg was caught by two edges of steel teeth. The teeth were covered in blood and the blood came from the old man's leg. Old Mali had stepped on a trap and his leg was caught firmly in the teeth of the trap. It was the same kind of trap that had caught the bear in Old Mali's story.

11

The Trap

I stood beside Old Mali who lay unconsciously[14] on the ground. I was too confused to do or say anything. I had now forgotten about the monkey.

At last I looked down and saw clearly what had happened. A hunter had prepared the trap many years before and left it. Then he had forgotten about it.

The trap was fixed to a log by a rusty piece of wire. The trap itself was old and rusty but it still looked strong. The teeth of the trap had bitten deeply into Old Mali's leg. It was the same leg that had been torn by the bear.

'Are you all right, Mali?' I asked. I tried to sound strong but I felt like crying.

'Are you all right?' I asked again.

Old Mali did not reply. He was lying unconscious on the ground and moaned a little from time to time. I felt really afraid. I was alone in the jungle.

'Mali,' I cried again. 'Mali, are you all right?'

Old Mali lay there and did not answer me. I looked round at the jungle, and I felt completely lost. What could I do? I did not know how to get back home and there was no one to help me.

Then Old Mali began to moan more loudly. He moved a little. Then, slowly, he moved his arm under his stomach. Moaning with the terrible pain in his leg, he turned himself round. Inch by inch he turned his body until he could sit up on the ground.

'Mali,' I cried again. 'Mali, are you all right?'

'You'll be all right, Mali,' I said, trying to make him feel better.

Old Mali did not listen to what I was saying. He looked at his leg caught in the trap. Then he looked carefully at the trap and the way in which it was fixed to the log.

'The same leg,' he said at last. 'It is the same leg.'

And I knew what he meant by these words. The trap had caught him on the same leg as the bear.

Old Mali lay back again. He seemed to be fighting off the terrible pain he was feeling in his leg. He sat up again, very slowly, after a few minutes. He turned a little and looked up at me.

'Do you remember,' Old Mali said at last, 'how I killed the bear when it was in the trap? Now it is *my* leg that is in the trap. And it's a strong trap too, even though it has been here for many years.'

'But it is old and rusty,' I replied quickly. 'Look at the wire round the log! I could easily cut that wire with my axe.'

'That would not help me,' replied Old Mali. 'I could never get back home pulling the heavy trap on my leg.'

Old Mali lay back again, moaning with pain. I looked at his leg and I saw the steel teeth biting into it. I saw the dark blood from his leg round the teeth of the trap. I felt that I wanted to be sick. I realized that Old Mali must be feeling really terrible pain.

Old Mali sat up and spoke to me with great difficulty.

'There is only one thing to do, Jeffa Baba,' he said. 'You must go home and bring help. Leave everything here that you don't need. Leave your rucksack and your bow and arrows. You will be able to go much more quickly if you do not carry all these things with you.'

I was too amazed at first to say anything. Old Mali did not understand how lost I was in the jungle. If I walked ten metres in the jungle without his help I would be completely lost. At last, I spoke.

'But I do not know the way,' I said simply. 'I do not know the way through the jungle.'

'Oh my father!' said Old Mali. 'This is bad luck from the monkey. What are we going to do now?'

Old Mali lay back for some time. He moaned from the pain in his leg and every now and again he whispered some words which I could not understand.

'Tomorrow is the third day,' he said to himself. 'I promised to return the boy on the third day. I must keep my promise.

'If only I had the little metal bar,' Old Mali whispered to himself later.

I knew what he was talking about. The little metal bar was a piece of metal carried by all hunters when they were using traps. They used the metal bar to open the teeth of the trap and free the animal's leg. If Old Mali had the metal bar, he could free his leg from the trap.

Then between his moans of pain, Old Mali began to talk about his leg. He said something about the leg being useless. The leg was no good for him and he must leave it behind in the jungle. But I did not understand what he meant.

At last Old Mali sat up again and turned to face me.

'Jeffa Baba,' he said, 'there is something that you must do for me. I want you to do exactly as I tell you. And do not ask me any questions.'

'I will do anything you want, Mali,' I replied without any hesitation.

'First of all, light a fire,' said Old Mali. 'Do not make a very big fire but make it very hot. When it is burning, put the blade of your *kukri* on the fire, until the blade is white-hot.'

'What is that for?' I asked curiously.

'Didn't you promise not to ask any questions?' Old Mali replied. He looked very tired. Then he lay back again moaning with pain.

I felt ashamed that I had troubled him. Then I began lighting a fire. When the fire was burning, I put the blade of my *kukri* on the fire.

'Is the fire lit yet?' Old Mali asked after a few minutes.

'Yes,' I replied quickly. 'The fire is lit and the *kukri* is getting hot.'

'Now you must do some heavy work,' Old Mali continued. 'Take my *kukri* and go and cut down a small tree. Choose a tree that is the thickness of your leg. When you have cut the tree down, cut from it a length of wood about one metre long. Then bring this log of wood over here.'

I did not understand at all why Old Mali wanted a log of wood, but I did not ask any more questions. Perhaps he had thought of some way to free his leg from the trap.

'I will cut the log much more quickly if I use the axe,' I said to Old Mali.

'No,' replied Old Mali. 'Take my *kukri*. We will need the axe later.'

Old Mali lay back on the ground again. He did not explain what we would need the axe for later. Then I took his *kukri* and went off to look for a suitable tree.

12

I Try to Free Old Mali

I soon found a tree that would give me a log about a metre long and the thickness of my leg. I began cutting the tree with Old Mali's *kukri*. It was hard work using a *kukri* instead of an axe. It took me some time to cut the tree down and cut off a log.

At last the log was cut and I picked it up and carried it on my shoulder. I laid it down beside Old Mali.

Old Mali was lying back on the ground still moaning with the pain. I had been frightened to look at his face. Now I looked at him and saw that his face was twisted with the most terrible pain. He was whispering to himself again as he moaned.

'I have promised,' Old Mali was saying, 'and I will keep my promise. I will return the boy on the third day.'

'I have brought the log of wood that you asked for,' I said, interrupting Old Mali. 'What do you want me to do with it?'

'Ah, you have returned,' said Old Mali, sitting up and looking at the log.

'Now, Jeffa Baba,' the old man continued, 'I want you to be very careful. You must lift the trap and move my leg so that it is straight. Then you must push the log under my leg and lay my leg down on the log.'

I stared back in horror when I heard these words. The very idea of touching Mali's leg horrified me. I stood and stared at the bloody leg. It was far too horrible to touch. I felt that I could never put my hands on that leg.

Old Mali was looking at me. I looked back at him and I could see a strange look in his eyes. He was trying to tell me that he understood my feeling of horror. But there was no time now to worry about such feelings. Old Mali stared at me in a frightening way. His eyes were ordering me to do what I had been told.

I moved forward and bent down. I touched the trap with one hand. The trap felt cold and horrible and I wanted to let go. I held the trap in my left hand and put my right hand under his leg.

I moved the trap forward and turned Old Mali's leg so that it was straight. When I turned the leg, Old Mali gave a great scream of pain. The scream frightened me so much that I nearly dropped the trap and the leg. But I held on to them carefully.

Still holding Old Mali's leg and the trap in the air, I slowly pushed the log under his leg. I held his leg gently and tried to push the log as carefully as I could. But I could not help twisting the leg from time to time. Every time I twisted his leg, Old Mali screamed with pain.

At last the log was lying under his leg just where Old Mali had said. I slowly lowered his leg until it was lying across the log. I raised my hands and stood back.

Old Mali must have felt terrible pain while I was moving his leg. When he spoke again, his voice was just a whisper.

'Go to the fire, Jeffa Baba,' Old Mali whispered, 'and see if the knife is hot yet.'

I went back to the fire and saw the steel blade was turning red. In a few moments the blade would be white-hot.

'The blade is almost white-hot,' I told him.

'And the axe?' Old Mali replied. 'Have you got the axe ready?'

'Yes,' I replied. 'I have the axe here.'

I stood waiting for the old man to speak again. I did not understand what he wanted me to do. I wondered what I had to do with the axe and the white-hot *kukri* blade.

After he had asked about the axe, Old Mali lay back on the ground again for a few moments. Then he sat up and looked straight at me.

'Jeffa Baba,' he said, 'we are in great trouble. I am going to die here in the jungle and you are going to die also.'

I looked at Mali with great surprise.

'No, no!' I cried strongly. 'I have my knife and the bow and arrows. We will not die.'

'Jeffa Baba,' repeated Old Mali, 'I tell you that we are going to die. We may die of hunger or thirst. But a worse death may come to us in the night.'

'I have my bow and arrows,' I said again.

'Your arrows will not help us,' continued Old Mali. 'In the night we may die a terrible death. All animals can smell blood. They will smell the blood from my leg. They will come here in

57

the night. If we have to stay here tonight, we will not be alive to see tomorrow morning.'

Old Mali was tired after speaking so much. He lay back breathing deeply and moaning with pain. After some time, he sat up again and continued.

'We must get away from here,' said Old Mali. 'And there is only one way for both of us to escape. I must leave some of my leg here in the trap.'

Old Mali had frightened me terribly. I remembered the night before in the jungle. On that night I had been frightened without any reason. To stay here for another night with Old Mali in the trap would be terrible.

'If I could do it myself,' Old Mali went on, 'I would. But I cannot do it lying here. It is you who must do it, Jeffa Baba. You must free me from this trap.'

'But how can I help you?' I replied, still not understanding what he wanted me to do.

'Listen to me carefully now,' said Old Mali. 'Can you remember how I taught you to cut the hardest wood with your axe?'

'Yes,' I replied. 'You told me that I must not think about the hardness of the wood. I must hit strongly at any piece of wood as if my axe will go straight through it.'

'That's right,' replied Old Mali eagerly. 'You must lift your axe, aim at the mark you want to hit and then hit that mark with all your strength.'

'Now, look here, Jeffa Baba,' said Old Mali, sitting right up and showing me his left leg. 'This is the mark you must aim at.'

He showed me a mark on his leg about an inch above the trap.

'You must free me from the trap by cutting through my leg,' said Old Mali simply. 'When you have cut through my leg, you must immediately bring the white-hot *kukri*. Put the *kukri* against my leg and that will stop the blood.'

At last I understood what Old Mali wanted me to do.

58

I had to cut through his leg. Then he would be free. I could not believe that he really wanted me to do such a terrible thing. I moved back in horror and the axe fell from my hand.

'*Sahib*,' said Old Mali suddenly.

Mali had never before called me *Sahib*. *Sahib* is an Indian word and it means master. Always, Mali had treated me like a child and called me Jeffa Baba. Now he was treating me like a man. He was calling me *Sahib*.

'*Sahib*,' said Old Mali, 'it is you who must do it. I cannot do it. It is you who must free me from the trap so that we can both live.'

Old Mali took out the piece of strong string that he always carried with him. He twisted the string round his leg just above the knee. He was doing exactly as he had said when he was telling the story of the trapped bear. He would tie the string tightly round his leg to stop the blood coming out. Now I really understood that he wanted me to cut his leg off.

'Now, *Sahib*, pick up the axe,' said Old Mali seriously and fiercely, 'and use it with all your strength.'

I tried to look away from Old Mali but I could not escape his eyes. They were burning like the eyes of a panther. His eyes were staring at me and telling me to pick up the axe.

I slowly picked up the axe and moved near to where Old Mali was lying. I raised the axe above my head. I aimed the axe at the mark on his leg.

I took a deep breath, and raising the axe as high as I could, I brought it down with all my strength. But at the last moment I was too frightened to watch the axe cutting into his leg. I closed both my eyes tightly.

There was a loud noise of steel hitting metal. I had missed Old Mali's leg and hit the trap. And as the axe hit the trap it twisted

*I slowly picked up the axe and moved near to where
Old Mali was lying.*

Old Mali's leg. He was lying back on the ground, unconscious.

I looked at his leg. It was still in the trap. I had not hit his leg at all. Instead I had hit the trap.

I looked down to see where the axe had hit the trap. And I suddenly noticed something different about it. On one edge of the trap the teeth were broken.

I had broken the trap. Old Mali was free. I did not have to cut his leg after all.

'Mali! Mali!' I cried, kneeling down beside him. 'It is finished. You are free.'

Old Mali lay unconscious on the ground. I shook him gently until his eyes began to open. Then I repeated the good news.

'You are free, Mali,' I told him excitedly.

Old Mali was not able to understand me at first. At last he was able to sit up. When he saw that his leg was still in the trap, he moaned sadly and lay back again.

'Jeffa Baba,' he whispered fiercely, 'are you not a man? You must try again. If we are both going to live, you must set me free. Pick up the axe and try again.'

'No, no!' I shouted. 'Sit up again and look. You are free. I have broken the trap.'

Old Mali slowly sat up again. He looked down at the trap. Whenever I looked at his leg, it still filled me with horror. But I knelt down beside his leg. I picked up the top piece of the trap which had broken and threw it away into the bushes.

Then I slowly lifted his leg. I had to pull quite strongly to get the teeth of the bottom piece of the trap out of his leg. When his leg was free from the teeth of the trap, I laid it gently on the ground. I stood up and pulled the trap as far away from Old Mali as possible.

When I had done this, I stood up and ran behind the tree. I knelt down and was terribly sick on the ground.

13

The Journey Home

I felt much better after I was sick. I went back to where Old Mali was still lying on the ground.

'Are you all right now' Old Mali asked me.

I told Old Mali that I felt better. But I still felt very weak.

'I must get a bandage for my leg,' said Old Mali. 'Have you anything in your rucksack that would make a bandage?'

'Will my blanket do?' I asked him.

'A blanket is too thick,' Old Mali replied. 'You must tear a piece off my shirt.'

'No, no, use mine,' I replied quickly.

I took off my shirt and tore it up into pieces. Old Mali sat up on the ground and tied the pieces tightly round his leg. When he had tied the bandage, Old Mali spoke to me again.

'Now you must cut some more wood, Jeffa Baba,' he said. 'I need two sticks. Go and cut two sticks so that they are long enough to reach from my shoulders to the ground. They will help me to walk the long way back home.'

I cut two sticks as Old Mali had told me. They had forks that fitted under Old Mali's arms. Before I gave them to Old Mali, I had an idea. I pulled my blanket out of the rucksack and tore two pieces from the blanket. I thought of my mother for a moment as I did so. She would be very angry to lose the blanket and the shirt.

Then I took the pieces of blanket and tied them round the forks of the sticks. When Old Mali put them under his arms, the pieces of blanket made the forks more comfortable. The forks would not hurt him so much when he was walking.

I packed everything in my rucksack and carried the axe and the bow in my left hand. The arrows were over my shoulder and the two *kukri's* were firmly in my belt.

When I had packed everything, I looked round. I would never forget that place in my life. The piece of broken trap lay still fixed to the log and the monkey was lying dead on the ground.

I thought of going up to the monkey to get back my arrow. But the sight of the monkey was too horrible for me. I still felt ready to be sick again. Also, the sight of the monkey reminded me that it was all my fault.

It was my fault that I had shot the monkey. If I had not shot the arrow at the monkey, Old Mali would not have gone back to kill it. If he had not gone back, his leg would not have got caught in the trap.

So it was all my fault.

Then I remembered something else. Everything that had happened on the journey was my fault. I had persuaded Old Mali to take me hunting with him. If we had not gone to hunt in the jungle, we would not have got into trouble and Old Mali's leg would be all right.

When I thought of the old man's leg, I wanted to cry. And when I remembered that it was all my fault, I began crying. But Old Mali quickly stopped me.

'Are we ready to move now?' asked Old Mali.

'Yes,' I replied. 'I have packed everything.'

'Then help me to stand up,' said the old man. I helped to lift up Old Mali. Then, I gave him the two sticks that I had cut for him. He put each of the sticks under his arms and then he began to move forward very slowly.

'Just like the time before,' said Old Mali.

I remembered the story of the trapped bear and his long, terrible journey back to his village. We had another long and terrible journey to make before we arrived home safely.

*He put each of the sticks under his arms and then he began to
move forward very slowly.*

14

A Sad End

We began walking together. I walked beside Old Mali to help him. Whenever we went up a slope, I walked in front. When I was in front, I turned around and faced Old Mali. Then, walking slowly backwards, I was able to put my hands on Old Mali's arms to help him up the slope.

But, in order to help him up a slope in this way, I had to have my hands free. This meant that I had to put the bow and the axe down on the ground at the bottom of each slope. When we reached the top of a slope, I had to leave Old Mali standing there. Then I went back down the slope, picked up the bow and the axe and climbed back up the slope again.

I often stopped to let Old Mali rest. I persuaded him once or twice to sit down. But after a few moments he was always eager to be off again.

'Tomorrow is the third day,' he repeated with great determination in his voice.

He was determined to get me back to Mother on the third day as he had promised. Even in his great pain and with such a terrible wound in his leg, Old Mali remembered his promise. He was thinking more of Mother and me than he was of himself.

We moved on slowly through the jungle. Sometimes, when the path became very narrow, I walked behind Old Mali. Then I saw his bandaged leg hanging uselessly. Blood was beginning to come through the bandage. Whenever I looked at it, I felt sick.

I was amazed at how brave Old Mali was. He must be feeling the most terrible pain. There was the pain from his leg and, also, the pain from the sticks under his arms. Even with the torn pieces of blanket the sticks still cut into his arms. Also, his hands must be tired holding up the weight of his body.

Luckily, I thought, Old Mali's hands were tough and strong. He had worked with them all his life. I had seen him using his hands in the garden day after day. His hands would not give him any pain.

It took us an hour and a half to reach the place where we had stopped the night before. We should have reached the place in half an hour but we were now moving very slowly through the jungle. We could not go any faster.

When we reached the place where we had stopped the night before, I helped Old Mali to lie down. I went and got some water from the stream. We both drank a lot of water.

'Give me some of my food from my bag,' Old Mali said.

I gave him some of his food. Old Mali sat up and forced the food into his mouth.

'You must eat something too, Jeffa Baba,' Old Mali told me.

I shook my head to show him that I did not want any food. I knew that I could not eat anything at all. If I had tried to eat I would have been sick again immediately.

I filled up the water bottle and after half an hour we began walking again. When I put the rucksack on my back again, it felt terribly heavy. 'Can I leave the axe here?' I asked Old Mali. 'I can come back and get it another day.'

Old Mali agreed.

I put the axe high up into a tree. I hoped that one day I would be able to come back to find the axe.

We moved on slowly through the jungle in silence. Old Mali was too tired to speak. I was thinking again about all the things that I had done wrong.

I thought of the happy days that Old Mali and I had had together. I remembered how he had taught me to fish and to catch snakes. We had had many happy days together. Old Mali had taught me so many things. And now it was all my fault that he was feeling such terrible pain.

I started to cry silently. I did not feel ashamed of crying. I felt that even a fully grown man should be allowed to cry when so much had gone wrong. I kept telling myself that it was all my fault.

As I walked in front of Old Mali, I was thinking of many things. Suddenly there was a loud noise behind me. Old Mali had slipped and fallen. He lay on the ground moaning with pain.

Again, I felt that it was my fault. I had been too busy thinking of myself and had forgotten about Old Mali. I rushed back and helped him to stand up.

'We must stop soon for the night,' said Old Mali. 'You must light a fire and make the beds before the sun goes down.'

We found a clearing. Old Mali rested on the ground while I lit a fire. When the fire was burning, I made beds of cryptomeria and moss for Old Mali and myself. I covered Old Mali's bed with the rest of my blanket and helped him to lie down on it.

I collected as much wood as possible before the sun went down. I made a pile of wood beside my bed so that I could keep the fire burning all night.

Just before I got into bed, I took the water bottle and had a long drink of water. I forgot completely that there was no stream near us. When I gave the water bottle to Old Mali, he looked at it. He drank a little and gave the bottle back to me.

'We must keep the rest of the water for tomorrow,' he said. 'There are no streams near the path that we must follow.'

I lay back on my bed and tried to sleep. Old Mali lay on his bed moaning from time to time. He was still worrying about Mother and me and his promise to get me back on the third day.

During the night, I kept putting some wood on the fire. The blackness of the jungle was all around me and it was full of the noises of animals. Strangely, the noises and the night in the jungle did not worry me. I had been so afraid when Old Mali was in the trap that there was no fear left in me.

At last I fell asleep. When I woke up in the morning, there was still some wood left in the pile that I had collected. And the fire was no longer burning.

We decided to leave immediately. I helped Old Mali out of bed and on to his sticks. We did not even take time to light the fire. We set off on our journey as soon as we got out of our beds.

Before we left, I made a big decision. I needed my hands completely free to help Old Mali. He was much weaker now than the day before. I decided that I would have to leave the bow in the jungle.

It was a difficult decision for me to make. I had wanted the bow so much. In fact it was the bow that had given me the idea of hunting in the jungle. And now I had to leave the bow behind.

I took out my *kukri* and made a big mark on a large tree that stood in the clearing. I put my bow and arrows at the bottom of the tree. And I promised myself that I would come back for the bow and arrows on another day.

Old Mali was becoming weaker all the time. He kept stopping and having a rest. Every time he sat down, I had to help him to stand up again. Each time I helped him up, it was more difficult. We went on and on through the jungle with the sun rising high in the sky.

It started to rain in the late afternoon. This made the ground slippery. Old Mali found it more difficult to use his sticks on the slippery ground. I walked beside him, helping him as much as I could.

Suddenly it happened before I could stop it. One stick slipped forward and Old Mali fell heavily to the ground. He fell down on top of his wounded leg and lay unconscious.

I shook him again and again until he started to moan and sit up. I tried to help him to stand up. He stood up holding his two sticks but immediately he fell down again. Now he was too weak to stand up.

'Help me up, again, *Sahib*,' he said to me in a very weak voice.

*Old Mali was becoming weaker all the time. Every time he sat
down, I had to help him to stand up again.*

Again I helped him to stand on his feet, but again he fell on the ground.

He lay there very tired and closed his eyes.

I did not know what to do. I was afraid that Old Mali would die and that we would never get home. In my fear, I began to be rude to him.

'Get up, Mali!' I shouted. 'Get up you lazy Indian.'

Old Mali did not understand me, but the noise of my voice made him open his eyes and sit up.

'The road,' Old Mali whispered, 'the road to your house is just behind that hill.'

I looked up at the hill and I felt excited. I recognized the part of the jungle that we were in. I knew where I was. Old Mali had succeeded. He would keep his promise to bring me back home on the third day.

I was so excited that I did not know what to do. Old Mali opened his eyes again and saw that I was still standing beside him. He thought that I had not understood him. Or he thought that I still did not know my way home.

'Crawl,' I heard Old Mali whisper to himself. 'I will show the boy the way by crawling.'

Although he was nearly too weak to move, Old Mali turned over on his stomach. He pushed his hands forward and started to crawl in the direction of the road. He was going to show me the way home. And as I watched him crawling I felt sad and angry.

'Stop, Mali, stop!' I cried out to him loudly. 'I know the way now. You have kept your promise. We will both be home on the third day. I will help you home.'

'No, no,' replied Old Mali weakly, 'leave me here. Go and tell your mother that you are all right. Bring help for me later.'

With these last words, Old Mali fell back on the ground unconscious.

I was determined not to leave him. He had wanted so much to get me home on the third day. I pulled the rucksack off my back and threw it to the ground. I bent down and using all my strength I was able to lift Old Mali upon my back across my shoulders.

When I staggered out onto the road, some villagers found me with Old Mali across my shoulders. They took us both to my home.

I was so ill that I had to lie in bed for three days. Every time I woke up, I asked whether Old Mali had recovered. Mother always replied, simply, that he was all right.

On the fourth day I felt much better and my mother told me what had happened.

When the villagers found me with Old Mali across my shoulders, he had already been dead for some time. He had probably died within a minute of me picking him up and carrying him. He had suffered no more from that terrible wound in his leg.

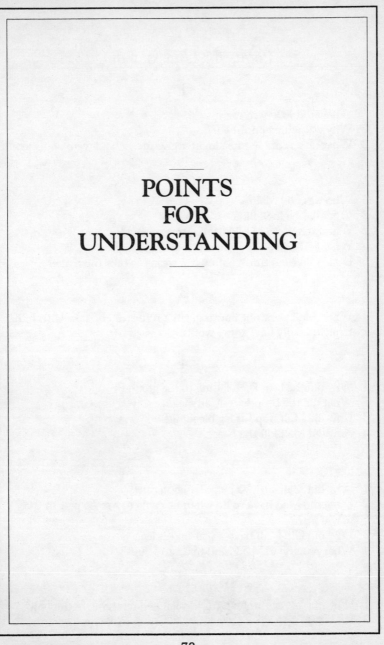

POINTS
FOR
UNDERSTANDING

Points for Understanding

1

1 Where did Jeffrey live?
2 Why was Jeffrey punished?
3 What reason did the headmaster give for such a severe punishment?

2

1 Who was Old Mali?
2 What did he look like?
3 What were most of Old Mali's stories about?
4 What had Old Mali promised to bring Jeffrey?
5 D   id Old Mali think Jeffrey was wrong to take the maize?

3

1 When Mali went out hunting, what things did he take with him?
2 Explain briefly how a trap works.

4

1 Why did the bear keep falling to the ground?
2 What did the bear do to Mali's leg?
3 How did Mali stop his leg bleeding?
4 How did Mali kill the bear?

5

1 Why did Mali cut two more bamboo canes?
2 What did Mali have to do when he came to a steep part in the jungle path?
3 Why did Old Mali have a scar on his leg?
4 What promise did Old Mali make to Jeffrey?

6

1 Why did Jeffrey think that Old Mali had not brought the bow?
2 Why did Old Mali want Jeffrey to learn to make his own arrows?

3 Why did they need a sharp knife before they went into the forest?
4 Why did Old Mali rub grease into the arrows?

7

1 Could Old Mali still use his bow?
2 What did Jeffrey want to do during the seven days' holiday?
3 What was Old Mali's reply when Jeffrey told him about his idea?

8

1 What persuaded Old Mali to take Jeffrey with him into the jungle?
2 Why did Old Mali think that they would not see more than five deer?
3 Why was Old Mali unusually worried when he was in the jungle with Jeffrey?

9

1 How had Old Mali learnt to do things in the jungle?
2 Why did Jeffrey not scream when he was afraid?
3 Why did Jeffrey jump out of bed when Old Mali made a noise?

10

1 Why did Jeffrey not ask Old Mali any questions?
2 Why did Jeffrey not want to go home?
3 What promise had Old Mali made to Jeffrey's mother?
4 Why was Old Mali very angry when Jeffrey shot the monkey?
5 What happened to Old Mali when he stepped forward towards the monkey?

11

1 What had happened earlier to the leg that Old Mali had now caught in the trap?
2 Would it help Old Mali if Jeffrey cut the wire that held the trap to the leg?
3 Why could Jeffrey not go back on his own to bring help?
4 What was Jeffrey to do with his *kukri* on the fire?
5 Why did Old Mali tell Jeffrey not to use the axe?

12

1 Why would Jeffrey not be able to keep the animals away during the night?
2 Why did Old Mali call Jeffrey Sahib?
3 What happened when the axe hit the trap?

13

1 Why did Old Mali ask Jeffrey to cut two sticks?
2 Why did Jeffrey start crying?
3 What did Old Mali mean by the words: 'Just like the time before'?

14

1 What happened to the bow?
2 Why was Jeffrey no longer afraid of being in the jungle at night?
3 What happened to Old Mali while Jeffrey was carrying him?
4 Had Old Mali kept his promise?
5 Give one example from any part of the story of:
   (a)   Old Mali's kindness
   (b)   Old Mali's bravery.

GLOSSARY

Glossary

1 *maize* (page 6)
   maize is a plant. It produces a large fruit called a cob. The cobs are covered with seeds which can be cooked and eaten.

2 *dormitory* (page 7)
   a large bedroom for the students who live at the school.

3 *bow* (page 8)
   a weapon made from a curved piece of wood with string or leather between the two ends. See the picture of a bow and arrow on page 13.

4 *beerie* (page 12)
   a roughly made cigarette. It is made by rolling up a tobacco leaf and tying it at one end with a piece of thread.

5 *kukri* (page 12)
   a long, sharp, curved knife. It can be used for hunting animals but it is also heavy enough for cutting thick sticks.

6 *dhoti* (page 12)
   a cloth worn round the waist. It hangs down to cover the legs. It is worn by some Indians, instead of trousers. See the illustration on page 13.

7 *clearing* (page 15)
   an open place in the jungle where there are no trees or bushes.

8 *grease* (page 17)
   fat from an animal's body.

9 *tear to pieces* (page 19)
   to pull something into small bits.

10 *within reach* – *out of reach* (page 20)
   something you can touch with your hands is within reach. Something you cannot touch is out of reach.

11 *stagger* (page 20)
   to move with difficulty, to be unable to use your legs properly.

12 *to keep a promise* (page 24)
   to do something that you have said you would do.

13 *cryptomeria* (page 31)
   a green bush which grows in the jungle.

14 *unconscious* (page 51)
   unable to speak, hear or do anything because you have been hit very hard or because you are very ill.

INTERMEDIATE LEVEL

Shane *by Jack Schaefer*
Old Mali and the Boy *by D. R. Sherman*
Bristol Murder *by Philip Prowse*
Tales of Goha *by Leslie Caplan*
The Smuggler *by Piers Plowright*
The Pearl *by John Steinbeck*
Things Fall Apart *by Chinua Achebe*
The Woman Who Disappeared *by Philip Prowse*
The Moon is Down *by John Steinbeck*
A Town Like Alice *by Nevil Shute*
The Queen of Death *by John Milne*
Walkabout *by James Vance Marshall*
Meet Me in Istanbul *by Richard Chisholm*
The Great Gatsby *by F. Scott Fitzgerald*
The Space Invaders *by Geoffrey Matthews*
My Cousin Rachel *by Daphne du Maurier*
I'm the King of the Castle *by Susan Hill*
Dracula *by Bram Stoker*
The Sign of Four *by Sir Arthur Conan Doyle*
The Speckled Band and Other Stories by *Sir Arthur Conan Doyle*
The Eye of the Tiger *by Wilbur Smith*
The Queen of Spades and Other Stories *by Aleksandr Pushkin*
The Diamond Hunters *by Wilbur Smith*
When Rain Clouds Gather *by Bessie Head*
Banker *by Dick Francis*
No Longer at Ease *by Chinua Achebe*
The Franchise Affair *by Josephine Tey*
The Case of the Lonely Lady *by John Milne*

For further information on the full selection of
Readers at all five levels in the series, please refer
to the Heinemann Readers catalogue.

Macmillan Heinemann English Language Teaching, Oxford

A Division of Macmillan Publishers Limited

Companies and Representatives all over the world

ISBN 0 435 27226 8

Heinemann is a registered trade mark of Reed Educational & Professional Publishing Ltd

© D. R. Sherman 1964
This retold version for Heinemann Guided Readers
© John Milne 1973, 1992
First published 1973
Reprinted four times
This edition published 1992

Illustrated by Peter Edwards
Typography by Adrian Hodgkins
Cover by Christopher Corr and Threefold Design
Typeset in 11/12.5 pt Goudy
by Joshua Associates Ltd, Oxford
Printed and bound in Great Britain by Cox and Wyman

98 99 00 01 02 10 9 8 7 6 5